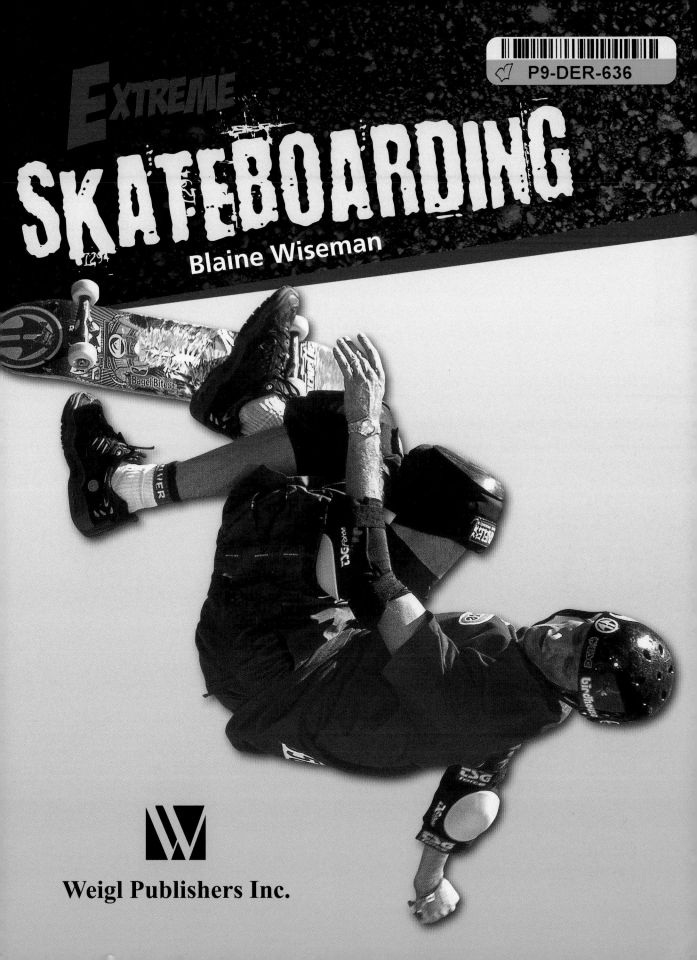

Extreme
SKATEBOARDING

Blaine Wiseman

Weigl Publishers Inc.

Published by Weigl Publishers Inc.
350 5th Avenue, Suite 3304, PMB 6G
New York, NY 10118-0069

Website: www.weigl.com
Copyright ©2009 WEIGL PUBLISHERS INC.

All of the Internet URLs given in the book were valid at the time of publication. However, due to the dynamic nature of the Internet, some addresses may have changed, or sites may have ceased to exist since publication. While the author and publisher regret any inconvenience this may cause readers, no responsibility for any such changes can be accepted by either the author or the publisher.

Library of Congress Cataloging-in-Publication Data available upon request.
Fax 1-866-44-WEIGL for the attention of the Publishing Records department.

ISBN 978-1-59036-912-8 (hard cover)
ISBN 978-1-59036-913-5 (soft cover)

Printed in the United States of America
2 3 4 5 6 7 8 9 0 12 11 10 09 08

Photo credits:
Weigl acknowledges Getty Images as its primary image supplier.
Other credits include: Andrew Guan, kickerclub.com: page 29 top right.

Every reasonable effort has been made to trace ownership and to obtain permission to reprint copyright material. The publishers would be pleased to have any errors or omissions brought to their attention so that they may be corrected in subsequent printings.

EDITOR: Heather C. Hudak
DESIGN: Terry Paulhus
LAYOUT: Kathryn Livingstone

EXTREME SKATEBOARDING

CONTENTS

WHAT ARE THE X GAMES?

The X Games are an annual sports tournament that showcases the best athletes in the extreme sports world. Extreme sports are performed at high speeds. Participants must wear special equipment to help protect them from injury. Only athletes who spend years training should take part in these sports. There are many competitions, such as the X Games, that celebrate the skill, dedication, and determination of the athletes, as well as the challenge and difficulty of the sports.

TECHNOLINK

Learn more about the X Games at **expn.go.com**.

The X Games began as the Extreme Games in 1995. The following year, the name was shortened to X Games. In 1995 and 1996, the games were held in the summer, and they featured a wide variety of sports. These included skateboarding, inline skating, BMX, street luge, sky surfing, and rock climbing.

The popularity of the X Games made it possible for more sports to be showcased. In 1997, the Winter X Games began. The Winter X Games feature sports such as snowboarding, skiing, and snowmobiling. Today, there are Summer and Winter X Games each year.

Some of the best skateboarders in the world compete in the X Games. These athletes perform extreme moves in front of large crowds. Events feature skaters flying 40 feet (12 meters) above the ground.

X FEST

The X Games are about more than sports. Each year, musical acts from all over the world perform for fans at the X Games. X Fest is the name for the musical portion of the X Games. It features some of the best-known punk rock, hip hop, and alternative music artists of the time. These artists perform between sporting events and keep the crowds entertained and excited for the competitions.

WHAT IS SKATEBOARDING?

Skateboarding is a sport that requires skill, determination, and balance. Skateboarders, or skaters, stand on the board and push themselves along with one foot. Shifting their weight from side to side turns the board. To stop, skaters drag their foot along the ground, flip the front of their board up to scrape the back on the ground, or turn very quickly so that they slide to a halt.

Skaters only are limited by their skill level and imagination. With practice, they can ride down stairs, grind rails and ledges, and jump over walls. Tricks can be difficult to learn. Many tricks are performed using ramps and jumps.

Timeline

1778 – European sailors observe native Hawai'ians riding boards on top of waves. The sport is called surfing.

1958 – Bill and Mark Richards begin using surfboards with wheels attached to ride on the streets.

1970s – Skaters begin using drained swimming pools for skateboarding. This was the beginning of **vert** style.

1973 – Frank Nasworthy starts Cadillac Wheels Company. The company makes wheels from urethane, a plastic that grips the ground better than clay wheels.

1975 – A team called the Z Boys introduces an **aggressive** style of skateboarding. This new style makes skateboarding one of the most popular sports in the United States.

In the late 1950s, skateboarders wanted to practice their moves when they were not in the water. Bill and Mark Richards, surfers from California, decided to try surfing on land. Richards attached wheels to boards and used them for sidewalk surfing. These boards were the first products sold as skateboards.

Skateboarding became popular in the 1970s, when a group from southern California changed the face of the sport. The Zephyr team, or the Z-Boys, from Venice Beach, California, developed a new style of skateboarding. They rode their boards lower to the ground and created many new tricks.

In 1978, Alan "Ollie" Gelfand changed the way people used their skateboards. He would stomp down on the back lip of his board and jump at the same time. This launched Alan and his board into the air. The trick was called the "ollie."

The ollie is used to perform almost every skateboarding trick, including rail grinding.

1976 – The world's first outdoor skateparks are built in Port Orange, Florida and Carlsbad, California.

1978 – Alan Gelfand invents the ollie. This move allows the skater and the board to leave the ground together.

1979 – Stacy Peralta of the Z Boys forms the Bones Brigade skateboard team. The team features many influential skaters, including Tony Hawk, Rodney Mullen, Allan Gelfand, Steve Caballero, and Bucky Lasek.

1995 – The first X Games take place, showcasing skateboarding to the world.

2002 – Skateboarding is brought to new heights by the Mega Ramp. This ramp launches skaters higher and farther than ever before.

ALL THE RIGHT EQUIPMENT

Traditionally, skateboarding has been an alternative sport. It has no set rules, and skaters are encouraged to be original and unique. This applies to clothing and behavior, as well as skating style and tricks.

Skaters often wear baggy clothes, including jeans, T-shirts, and hooded sweatshirts. Baggy clothes allow more movement when performing tricks. Many skaters wear shoes made just for skateboarding. These shoes have flat soles and special grips that help with jumping and turning.

Even the best skaters in the world fall often, so when starting out, skaters must be ready to take their fair share of falls. Skateboarding is done on hard surfaces, such as wood or concrete. This means that skaters must wear the proper equipment to protect themselves if they fall.

ACCESSORIZE IT!

While some boards are sold assembled, most skateboard pieces are sold separately. They are assembled by the skater. This makes it possible for skaters to choose their own parts and make the board unique. The topside of the board is often covered in black grip tape. This kind of tape feels like sandpaper. It helps the skater's shoes grip the board when performing stunts.

The helmet is the most important piece of safety equipment. When falling off a skateboard, a skater's head can hit the ground. Helmets have saved many skaters from serious head injuries.

Many skaters wear knee and elbow pads. Skaters learn how to use these pads as cushions. Skaters can break their wrists if they brace themselves with their hands when they fall. Instead of using their hands, skaters can fall on their elbows or knees, which are protected by pads.

The most important piece of equipment in skateboarding is the skateboard. Skateboards often are made of maple wood. Common boards used in competitions curve upwards at both ends. This is so that skaters can perform **aerial** tricks without their feet slipping off the sides of the board.

The bottom side of the board has four wheels, two in front and two at the back. Most often, the wheels are made of polyurethane, a special type of rubber. The metal pieces that attach the wheels to the board are called trucks. These are made of metal, such as aluminum or steel.

SURVEYING THE VENUE

Skateboarding can be done almost anywhere there is concrete, pavement, metal, stone, or wood. Sidewalks and city streets are perfect for freestyle skaters who want to explore their surroundings. They can ride walls, curbs, and ledges. They also can grind their wheels on rails or perform flip tricks on flat land. Almost anything can be used as an obstacle. Common obstacles for jumping over are garbage cans, traffic cones, benches, and other skateboards. Gaps between surfaces are good for jumping as well.

Skateparks are special areas made for skateboarding. These often have concrete or wooden ramps and jumps. Skateparks may include railings, **halfpipes**, **quarterpipes**, and other obstacles and ramps.

The X Games use different types of courses depending on the event. Each has its own share of obstacles. One competition takes place on a huge ramp that launches the skater over a 70-foot (21-m) gap. If the skater lands this trick successfully, he or she then rides up a 27-foot (8-m) quarterpipe. Another competition takes place on a halfpipe. The final competition allows skaters to use obstacles such as ramps, rails, and staircases.

Many tricks can be performed by jumping off a halfpipe or quarterpipe.

TECHNOLINK

To find out how to build
a skatepark in your city,
visit **www.spausa.org**.

BIG AIR

The most extreme skateboarding competition in the X Games is called Big Air. This competition begins with the skater riding down an 80-foot (24-m) ramp and launching over a 70-foot (21-m) gap. After landing the jump over the gap, the skater then rides up a 27-foot-(8-m-) high quarterpipe. At the top, the skater continues over the edge, shooting straight into the air. Skaters can perform a variety of tricks in the Big Air competition, including flip tricks, grabs, spins, and even backflips.

Danny Way built the first Mega Ramp in 2002.

The Big Air competition was first introduced to the X Games in 2004. Professional skater Danny Way developed the Mega Ramp to launch skaters over the gap. Way won the first Big Air gold medal and broke his own world record for the longest distance jumped on a skateboard—79 feet (24 m).

Big Air is a best trick contest. This means that the skater who performs the most impressive trick wins the event. Each skater takes five runs, and they are judged on **amplitude**, difficulty of the trick, and style. To have good style, the skater must make the trick look as effortless as possible and land it comfortably. Crashing, wobbling after landing, or spinning out of control in the air can take away style points.

BIG AIR
PAST WINNERS

2007
Gold – Bob Burnquist
Silver – Jake Brown
Bronze – Pierre-Luc Gagnon

2006
Gold – Danny Way
Silver – Jake Brown
Bronze – Bob Burnquist

VERT

The Vert competition has been a part of the X Games from the beginning. This competition takes place on a 120-foot- (37-m-) wide, 11-foot- (3-m-) high halfpipe. Skaters ride from the top of one side of the halfpipe to the top of the other in a continuous motion. During their run, skaters perform a mixture of aerial, or big air, and technical tricks when they reach the top of the ramp. There are Vert competitions for both men and women.

Each rider gets three 45-second runs to perform a series of different stunts. The runs are judged based on style, aggressive **execution**, difficulty, variety of tricks, amplitude, continuity of the run, and use of the ramp. Six judges score for each run. The highest and lowest scores are not included in the final score.

The final score is based on the average of the remaining four scores. The skater with the highest single score out of the three runs wins the competition. The winner often includes aerial grabs, spins and flip tricks, and technical tricks, such as grinds, **stalls**, and **boardslides** as part of his or her routine.

Steve Caballero won silver at the X Games in Sydney, Australia, in 2001.

Alex Perelson was only 16 years old when he took part in X Games 13.

VERT PAST WINNERS

2007
Men's Gold – Shaun White
Men's Silver – Pierre-Luc Gagnon
Men's Bronze – Mathias Ringstrom

2007
Women's Gold – Lyn-Z Adams Hawkins
Women's Silver – Mimi Knoop
Women's Bronze – Cara-Beth Burnside

STREET

The X Games street competition has been featured since the first Extreme Games in 1995. Skaters compete in a special skatepark that consists of ramps, stairs, rails, ledges, boxes, and other obstacles. Each competitor takes three timed runs through the park. Skaters can use any of the obstacles as many times as they want. They are judged on aggressive execution, style, difficulty, variety, originality, and number of tricks performed, as well as on their use of the park. Skaters receive higher scores if they use a different obstacle for each trick, perform multiple tricks quickly without much time in between, and perform difficult tricks.

Street is a highly technical skateboarding competition. Skaters perform small jumps, grinds, and flip tricks. The event features both men's and women's competitions.

Dayne Brummet took part in X Games 8 in Philadelphia, Pennsylvania.

17

QUALIFYING TO COMPETE

The first step to becoming a professional skater is getting a sponsorship. This means that a company will pay a person money to represent them, supply free clothing and equipment, or pay transportation costs to tournaments and events. To get sponsored, a person must be very good at skateboarding.

Practice is the most important part of becoming good at any sport. Most professional skaters spend several hours every day skateboarding. They push themselves to try new and difficult tricks. They explore different places, including parks, cities, and countries. By doing this, skaters find obstacles that they have never tried before. This forces them to try new moves and improve their skating.

TECHNOLINK

To learn more about getting sponsored, check out **www.kidzworld.com/article /1770-skateboarding-how-to-get-sponsored**.

Once skaters have developed their skills, they are ready to seek sponsors. This is done by making contact with companies. Most skateboard companies have information for getting sponsored on their websites.

To qualify for the X Games, a skater must compete in certain other events throughout the year, including various World Cup competitions. The top skaters in each competition qualify automatically for the X Games. The top skaters in the overall standings of World Cup Skateboarding also qualify. To rank at the top of the standings, a skater must compete in most of the competitions and rank near the top in all of them.

SIMILAR SPORTS

While skateboarding is a unique sport that is popular around the world, it is not the only sport in which the athlete rides a board. These sports are similar to skateboarding.

Wakeboarding

Wakeboarding was developed from surfing and water skiing. Like surfing, the athlete rides a board in the water. However, instead of riding on waves, the rider holds onto a rope that is attached to a motorboat. The boat tows the wakeboarder through the water at high speeds. The rider uses the wake as a jump and performs aerial stunts behind the boat.

Wakeboarding can be done on almost any smooth body of water where motorboats are allowed. Some of the best places for wakeboarding are California, Costa Rica, Australia, and Greece.

Surfing

Surfing is a sport where the athlete stands on a board and rides a wave of water. It is the model for all other board sports today. People surf in many places all over the world. All they need are powerful, rolling waves and a surfboard. Most people surf in powerful ocean breaks. Some of the most common places for surfing are Hawai'i, California, Australia, and Brazil.

Snowboarding

Snowboarding is a combination of surfing and skiing. The athlete rides a board down a snow-covered hill. Snowboarders travel at very high speeds, so the board is attached to their feet with **bindings**. World-class snowboarding hills can be found in Utah, the Canadian Rockies, the Swiss Alps, and the mountains of New Zealand.

Kiteboarding

Kiteboarding is a sport where athletes are tied to a specially designed kite, while their feet are strapped to a board. The kites are designed to catch much more wind than normal kites. This means that the athlete can be pulled along at speeds up to 48 **knots** per hour. Kiteboarding is most commonly done on water, like surfing. However, kiteboards can also be ridden on snow, dirt, and pavement.

UNFORGETTABLE MOMENTS

Throughout the history of the X Games, there have been many unforgettable moments. These include record-breaking wins, long falls, and new tricks.

At the 1999 X Games in San Francisco, Tony Hawk, one of the best-known skaters in history, landed a trick that had never been landed before. During the best trick competition, Hawk flew above the halfpipe. He spun his body and board two-and-a-half times. The trick is called a 900 because Hawk spun 900 degrees. After landing the trick, Hawk said, "This is the best day of my life… What else is there? The 900 was my goal."

Two years later, in San Francisco, Bob Burnquist won gold in the Vert competition, with the greatest run in X Games history. Burnquist was the final competitor and sat in second place behind the two-time defending champion, Bucky Lasek. The final run included many tricks that had never been seen before. They were so new that they did not even have names. Burnquist was rewarded with the highest score ever given at the X Games—98.

In 2007, at the X Games in Los Angeles, Australian skater Jake Brown survived the longest fall in X Games history. During the Big Air competition, Brown landed a perfect 720, spinning two full rotations over the 70-foot (21-m) gap. As he continued on to the quarterpipe, Brown began to lose control of his board. After launching above the ramp, Brown fell away from his board and fell about 45 feet (14 m). The fall was so forceful that Brown's shoes flew off his feet.

After lying motionless on the ground for nearly five minutes, Brown walked away with help from paramedics. He suffered a broken wrist and a bruised lung.

AROUND THE WORLD

Vancouver, Canada

Vancouver offers a large number of skateparks, both indoor and outdoor. There are also many ledges, rails, staircases, and jumps throughout the city.

ATLANTIC OCEAN

Sao Paulo, Brazil

Sao Paulo has many great places to skate, including large parks, a huge downtown area full of ledges, rails, and jumps, and more than 40 public ramps throughout the city.

PACIFIC OCEAN

San Francisco, United States

San Francisco is one of the most popular cities in North America for skateboarding. The warm weather makes it perfect for skating most days of the year. The winding, hilly city streets are the main attraction for skaters in San Francisco. These offer many different obstacles for all levels of skaters.

X Games Venues

1. Rhode Island, United States
2. Los Angeles, United States
3. Mexico City, Mexico
4. Rio de Janeiro, Brazil
5. Kuala Lumpur, Malaysia
6. Shanghai, China

ARCTIC
OCEAN

ARCTIC
OCEAN

Frankfurt, Germany

Frankfurt is a city of office buildings and skyscrapers. The architecture of the city offers a wide variety of street skating spots.

Barcelona, Spain

Barcelona is known as the "Skate Capital of the World." City officials have embraced skateboarding and allow it at many public places, including art museums, markets, and train stations.

PACIFIC
OCEAN

INDIAN
OCEAN

Melbourne, Australia

Melbourne's streets are loaded with obstacles. Melbourne also has many indoor and outdoor skateparks available to the public.

CURRENT STARS

ELISSA STEAMER

HOMETOWN
Fort Myers, Florida, United States

BORN
July 31, 1975

NOTES
First female to have a skateboard shoe and **deck** designed for her

Won the first women's street competition in 1998 in Vancouver

Has won the Slam City Jam, X Games, Gravity Games, and World Cup Skateboarding competitions

RYAN SHECKLER

HOMETOWN
San Clemente, California, United States

BORN
December 30, 1989

NOTES
Began skateboarding at 18 months of age

Turned professional when he was 14 years old

Has won many awards, including World Cup of Skateboarding National Street Champion, X Games medals, and Gravity Games medals

BOB BURNQUIST

HOMETOWN
Sao Paulo, Brazil

BORN
October 10, 1976

NOTES
Turned professional at 14 years old, only three years after skateboarding for the first time

Won *Thrasher* magazine's Skater of the Year award in 1997

Has won X Games gold medals in Vert, Vert doubles, and Big Air

CHRIS COLE

HOMETOWN
Levittown, Pennsylvania, United States

BORN
March 10, 1982

NOTES
Had his first skateboard shoe designed in 2005

Has won awards at the X Games, Gravity Games, and many other competitions

Is known for being able to skate **switch** and **regular**

LEGENDS

TONY HAWK

HOMETOWN
San Diego, California, United States

BORN
May 12, 1968

NOTES
Began skateboarding when his brother gave him a board for his ninth birthday

Has won 16 X Games medals in Vert competitions, including 10 gold

Has invented more than 80 tricks and is considered by many to be the greatest skater in history

TONY ALVA

HOMETOWN
Santa Monica, California, United States

BORN
September 2, 1957

NOTES
Skated with the Zephyr team in the 1970s

Was the first skater to perform an aerial stunt—a **frontside air**

Started his own skateboard company, Alva Skates, at age 19

STACY PERALTA

HOMETOWN
Santa Monica, California, United States

BORN
October 15, 1957

NOTES
Skated with the Zephyr team in the 1970s

Started the Powell-Peralta Skateboard Company and the Bones Brigade skate team

Was a professional skater and a surfer and is now a television and film director

RODNEY MULLEN

HOMETOWN
Redondo Beach, California, United States

BORN
August 17, 1966

NOTES
Is credited with inventing most skateboard flip tricks, including the **kickflip** and **heelflip**

Skated with the Powell-Peralta Bones Brigade, alongside Ollie Gelfand, Tony Hawk, Colin McKay, and Stacy Peralta

Founded World Industries and Almost, two successful skateboard companies

THE 10 QUESTION QUIZ

1. In what year were the first X Games held?

2. What was skateboarding originally called?

3. What team turned skateboarding into an extreme sport?

4. What are the three skateboarding events at the X Games?

5. Who invented the Mega Ramp?

6. Name four sports that are similar to skateboarding.

7. How many rotations must a skater make to complete a 900?

8. What city is the "Skate Capital of the World"?

9. Who performed the first aerial stunt off a ramp?

10. What skateboard team was started by Stacy Peralta?

Answers: 1. 1995 2. Sidewalk Surfing 3. Zephyr Team or Z-Boys 4. Big Air, Vert, and Street 5. Danny Way 6. Surfing, snowboarding, kiteboarding, and wakeboarding 7. Two-and-a-half 8. Barcelona, Spain 9. Tony Alva 10. Bones Brigade

RESEARCH

www.expn.go.com

www.expn.go.com/skt

www.kidzworld.com/article/1829-build-your-own-skatepark

www.drskateboard.com

Many books and websites provide information on skateboarding. To learn more, borrow books from the library, or surf the Internet.

Most libraries have computers that connect to a database for researching information. If you input a keyword, you will be provided with a list of books in the library that contain information on that topic. Nonfiction books are arranged numerically, using their call number. Fiction books are organized alphabetically by the author's last name.

GLOSSARY

aerial: taking place in the air

aggressive: to do something with extra effort

amplitude: to be very large

bindings: fasteners used to hold something in place

boardslides: the rider slides with his or her board sideways and in the center of an obstacle

deck: the wooden part of the board

execution: the carrying out of an action and the quality of that action

frontside air: a trick done in the air when the rider is facing the obstacle

halfpipes: two ramps that curve inward and are facing each other with an area of flat ground between them

heelflip: to kick the board with the toe

kickflip: to kick the board into a spin before landing on it

knots: measurements of speed for travel done on a body of water

quarterpipes: single ramps that curve inward

regular: to ride with the left foot forward

stalls: to place the board in the same way as if doing a grind or slide, but without moving

switch: to ride with the opposite foot forward

vert: a type of skateboarding that is done on ramps that includes trips and jumps

INDEX